How to Play Table Tennis for Beginners

The Ultimate Guide to Mastering Everything from Rules, Racket Techniques, and Etiquette to Serve, Scoring, and Tips for Single and Doubles

© **Copyright 2023 - All rights reserved.**

The content contained within this book may not be reproduced, duplicated, or transmitted without direct written permission from the author or the publisher.

Under no circumstances will any blame or legal responsibility be held against the publisher, or author, for any damages, reparation, or monetary loss due to the information contained within this book, either directly or indirectly.

Legal Notice:

This book is copyright protected. It is only for personal use. You cannot amend, distribute, sell, use, quote, or paraphrase any part of the content within this book without the consent of the author or publisher.

Disclaimer Notice:

Please note the information contained within this document is for educational and entertainment purposes only. All effort has been executed to present accurate, up-to-date, reliable, and complete information. No warranties of any kind are declared or implied. Readers acknowledge that the author is not engaging in the rendering of legal, financial, medical, or professional advice. The content within this book has been derived from various sources. Please consult a licensed professional before attempting any techniques outlined in this book.

By reading this document, the reader agrees that under no circumstances is the author responsible for any losses, direct or indirect, that are incurred as a result of the use of the information contained within this document, including, but not limited to, errors, omissions, or inaccuracies.

Table of Contents

Introduction 1

Chapter 1: Getting Started 3

Chapter 2: Essential Equipment 14

Chapter 3: Grips and Strokes 25

Chapter 4: Serving and Receiving 41

Chapter 5: Singles Play 49

Chapter 6: Doubles Play 56

Chapter 7: Scoring and Keeping Tracks 65

Chapter 8: Improving Your Game 71

Conclusion 79

References 82

Introduction

Table tennis is a game where speed, precision, and strategy unite in an exhilarating dance across a tiny table. If you've ever been captivated by the lightning-fast rallies and dreamed of mastering the art of table tennis, you're in for an exciting journey. "How to Play Table Tennis for Beginners" is your passport to unlocking the secrets of this fascinating sport, designed explicitly for newcomers eager to grasp the fundamentals, improve their skills, and savor the game.

This book is your coach, mentor, and guide, dedicated to making you the table tennis player you've always wanted to be. It aims to empower beginners with the knowledge, techniques, and confidence to play like a seasoned pro. Whether you're a complete novice or have dabbled in the sport, this book is tailored for you. It demystifies the complexities of table tennis, breaking down the game into simple, actionable steps that ensure not just comprehension but also tangible progress.

What Sets This Book Apart

In a crowded market of table tennis guides, "How to Play Table Tennis for Beginners" stands out as the go-to choice for one simple reason. It's all about you, the beginner. Here's why this book is a cut above the rest:

- **Crystal Clear and Beginner-Friendly:** Complex table tennis techniques are made simple and understandable. There is no jargon or confusion—just straightforward explanations.

- **Hands-on Learning:** This book doesn't just tell you what to do but shows you how to do it. Step-by-step instructions and hands-on methods ensure you can effortlessly apply the techniques, helping you improve your game with every practice session.

- **Built for Beginners:** Unlike many guides that assume prior knowledge, this book starts from the basics. It assumes nothing and guides you from the ground up, making it informative and empowering for those just beginning.

- **Comprehensive Approach:** From the fundamental rules to advanced strategies, this book is your one-stop resource for all things table tennis. It covers everything you need to know to become a proficient table tennis player.

- **Engaging and Inspirational:** Forget dry manuals. This book reads like a conversation with a supportive coach. It has engaging anecdotes, motivational stories, and inspirational examples encouraging you to push your limits and aim for excellence.

Picture yourself with the paddle, confidently taking on opponents in a high-stakes table tennis showdown. This guide is your ticket to making that dream a thrilling reality. If you're eager to start this exhilarating journey, turn the pages and unlock a world where passion meets practice and your table tennis aspirations become achievements.

Chapter 1: Getting Started

Table tennis is a fast-paced and exhilarating sport enjoyed by people of all ages and skill levels. If you're new to this game, this exciting journey promises hours of fun and the opportunity to improve your coordination, reflexes, and overall fitness. Whether you've never held a paddle before or are simply looking to brush up on the basics, this chapter is your gateway to getting started.

The Rich History of Table Tennis

1. Table tennis is a game with a rich history. Source: https://unsplash.com/photos/two-men-playing-ping-pong-inside-room-dybZ3jXtYUo?utm_content=creditShareLink&utm_medium=referral&utm_source=unsplash

Table tennis, also affectionately known as ping pong, is a sport that has brought joy, competition, and camaraderie to millions worldwide. It's a game of lightning-fast reflexes and precision, played on a small table with a lightweight ball and paddles. But many may not realize that table tennis's history is a fascinating tale of transformation from a parlor game to a global phenomenon.

Origins: From Parlor Game to Competitive Sport

Table tennis has its roots in England, where it was initially a parlor game for the upper class during the late 19th century. Back then, it went by names such as "whiff-whaff" and "gossima." These early versions used various materials for balls, including Champagne corks, which were favored for their bounce.

The first table tennis sets appeared in the 1880s, using celluloid balls and improvised paddles. These early versions resembled lawn tennis and were played indoors during inclement weather. It wasn't long before the game became popular and spread to other countries.

The Birth of an Official Sport

Table tennis made its way to other parts of Europe and Asia, but it was only in 1926 that the game saw its first international championship. The International Table Tennis Federation (ITTF) was founded, which marked the formal recognition of table tennis as a competitive sport.

The first World Table Tennis Championships were held in London, attracting players worldwide. It was here that the sport was officially named "table tennis," a term that had been in informal use but was now cemented in history.

The Chinese Dominance

In the latter part of the 20th century and into the 21st century, China became a powerhouse in table tennis. Chinese players dominated international competitions, consistently taking home the gold medals at the Olympics, World Championships, and other major tournaments. China's rise in table tennis is a testament to the country's dedication, rigorous training, and unmatched talent in the sport.

Table Tennis at the Olympics

Table tennis made its Olympic debut in 1988 during the Seoul Summer Olympics. The sport has since become a staple of the Olympic program, with singles and team events for both men and women. Olympic table tennis matches have brought new excitement to the sport, with the world's best athletes competing on the grandest stage.

The Evolution of Equipment

Table tennis equipment has also come a long way. The original paddles were made of wood and often had leather or pimpled rubber on one side. The balls were initially celluloid, but they transitioned to plastic in recent years due to safety and environmental concerns.

The evolution of the rubber on paddles has added an exciting dimension to the game. Different types of rubber can provide spin, speed, or control, allowing players to tailor their equipment to their playing style.

The Thrill of Modern Table Tennis

Today, table tennis is not just a leisure activity—it's a global phenomenon. The sport boasts a vibrant professional circuit with athletes who command respect and admiration. It's a game of precision, strategy, and split-second decision-making. Furthermore, table tennis has retained its accessibility. You can find tables in parks, recreation centers, and even homes. The game's simplicity allows beginners to get started quickly while offering challenges to those who wish to master the art of spin, speed, and control.

The rich history of table tennis takes us on a journey from its parlor game origins to becoming a global sensation. It's a story of evolution, dedication, and international unity. As you pick up your paddle and stand by the table, remember that you are a part of a sport with a vibrant history and a thrilling future.

The Appeal of Table Tennis

Table tennis has a universal charm that transcends age and skill levels. Here are some reasons why it's such a beloved sport:

- **Accessibility:** One of the most significant advantages of table tennis is its accessibility. You don't need a massive field, expensive equipment, or a large group of people to enjoy a game. A table, paddles, and a partner are all you need.

- **Physical Fitness:** Despite its small size, table tennis offers a fantastic cardiovascular workout. The fast-paced rallies and constant movement help improve agility, coordination, and reflexes.

- **Mental Stimulation:** Table tennis is as much a mental sport as a physical one. Players need to strategize, anticipate their opponent's moves, and adjust to changing game dynamics.

- **Social Interaction:** Whether playing casually with friends or participating in local tournaments, table tennis is an excellent way to meet new people and build connections.

- **Competitive Spirit:** For those with a competitive edge, table tennis offers a thriving competitive scene. From local clubs to international championships, ample opportunities exist to test your skills and aim for glory.

Table tennis, or ping pong, is more than just a casual game you might play in a basement or recreation room. It's a sport with a rich history, straightforward rules, and an enduring appeal, making it a fantastic pastime for people of all ages and backgrounds. Enjoy the fast-paced action and the camaraderie it brings, and who knows, you might find yourself falling in love with this thrilling game.

The Game in a Nutshell

Table tennis is like a game of tennis but on a pint-sized scale. The idea is to keep the ball moving back and forth over the net, landing it on your opponent's side without them being able to hit it back to yours. Before you jump into the details, here's a quick peek at the basics.

The Essentials: Table Tennis Equipment

2. *To get started with table tennis, you need to have a table, a paddle, and a ball. Source: https://unsplash.com/photos/red-and-brown-wooden-table-tennis-racket-iokB5B9J8Ds?utm_content=creditShareLink&utm_medium=referral&utm_source=unsplash*

To get started with table tennis, you'll need a few key pieces of equipment:

1. **The Table:** The table is a rectangular playing surface divided into two halves by a net. It measures 9 feet in length, 5 feet in width, and stands 2.5 feet above the ground.

2. **The Paddle (or Racket):** The paddle is your primary tool for hitting the ball. It's usually made of wood and covered with rubber on both sides. One side of the rubber is red, and the other is black. These colors are used for differentiating spin on the ball.

3. **The Ball:** The ball is small and lightweight, measuring 40 mm in diameter. It's typically made of celluloid or plastic.

Service Rules

The serve is the grand opener of any ping-pong battle. Prepare to serve up some excitement as you uncover the secrets of the perfect ping-pong launch!

- **The Toss:** The server tosses the ball to get the game started. But this isn't just any toss. It has to be at least 6 inches high and visible to the receiver. No magic tricks are allowed here!

- **The Point of Contact:** Don't get too fancy when you serve. Hit the ball with your paddle in an open palm, keeping your hand steady as a rock.

- **The Ball's Path:** Your mission as the server is to send the ball diagonally to the receiver's side. The ball must bounce on your side before it clears the net and lands on their side.

Mastering the serve sets the tone for the entire game, adding an element of surprise and strategy to your gameplay. So, next time you step up to serve, remember the toss, the contact, and the path, and watch your opponents marvel at your ping-pong prowess!

Rally Rules

The rally is where lightning-fast exchanges and quick thinking reign supreme. Get ready to hone your reflexes and rally like a champ.

1. **Ball Bouncing:** After the serve, the ball must bounce on your side of the table before you hit it—volleys are not allowed in table tennis. This rule keeps things fair and square for both players.

2. **Volleys:** Volleys are illegal, meaning you can't go for a slam dunk before the ball bounces on your side. You'll lose a point if you volley the ball back to your opponent.

3. **Points Scoring:** Here's how you score points in ping pong:

- Your opponent misses the ball after you play a legal shot.
- Your opponent hits the ball into the net.
- The opponent returns the ball, but it misses your side of the table.
- The ball is hit by your opponent's body instead of, or as well as, the paddle.
- There are other subtle ways a point can be won, but these constitute 99% of points.

Rallies are the heartbeat of table tennis, where players showcase their skills and adaptability. Perfecting the bounce and embracing the art of volleys can turn the tide of any match, making you a formidable opponent. Practice your moves, watch the ball, and prepare to dominate the ping pong court.

Table Tennis Etiquette

Beyond the rules, sportsmanship and respect are the cornerstones of table tennis. Get ready to learn how to be a gracious winner and a humble loser, essential traits of a true ping pong champion.

- **Sportsmanship:** Shake hands with your opponent before and after the game. It shows respect and keeps the environment friendly.
- **Prompt Play:** Nobody likes a slowpoke. Play with speed when needed in the game, but don't hesitate on your

serve either. Play at a regular tempo at all times—speed adds a zing to the game.

- **Noise Control:** Keep the chitchat and cheering to a minimum, especially when your opponent is serving. It's all about respecting the focus.

- **Adherence to Rules:** Follow the rules and respect the referee's decisions. If there's a disagreement, settle it with a friendly game of "rock-paper-scissors."

- **Stay Positive:** Ping pong can get intense, and losing points is part of the game. Stay positive, keep your cool, and focus on improving your game. Celebrate your victories and be graceful in defeat.

- **Equipment Care:** Treat your paddle and the table with love. Slamming your paddle and roughhousing are big no-nos. Keep it clean, maintain your gear, and it will serve you well.

Table tennis etiquette reflects your love for the game and for your opponent. Embracing sportsmanship, prompt play, and positivity creates an enjoyable atmosphere on the table, ensuring that every game is not just a match but a memorable experience. Remember your manners, keep the game lively, and let the good times roll on the table.

Table Tennis Game Variations: Adding Spice to Your Ping Pong

Table tennis, with its lightning-fast rallies and thrilling gameplay, is a sport that offers immense flexibility and adaptability. Beyond the standard rules, numerous variations add a unique twist to the classic ping-pong experience. These adaptations allow players to customize the game to their preferences and skill levels.

Singles and Doubles Play

The most common distinction in table tennis is between singles and doubles. In singles, it's one player against another, while doubles involves two players on each side. Doubles introduces teamwork and strategic coordination, making it a fantastic way to enjoy the game with friends or family. It's also an excellent option for those looking to improve their social connections.

Round the World

Round the World, also known as "Ping Pong Around the World," is a fun and casual table tennis variation. In this game, players take turns hitting the ball to predetermined spots on the table, attempting to land it in each spot. It's an excellent way to practice precision and ball control while enjoying a more relaxed social game.

Round Robin Tournament

Organizing a Round Robin Tournament can be a blast if you have a group of ping-pong enthusiasts. In this format, each player or team competes against every other player or team in a round-robin fashion. Points are awarded for wins and draws, and the player or team with the most points emerges as the champion. It's a fantastic way to encourage healthy competition and engage with multiple opponents.

Backhand Serve Challenge

The Backhand Serve Challenge is an exciting variation that focuses on serving techniques. In this game, players take turns serving by using only their backhand, which can be more challenging than the typical forehand serve. It's an excellent exercise for refining your backhand skills and adapting to different serving styles.

Speed Ping Pong

Speed Ping Pong is the perfect choice for those seeking an adrenaline rush. In this variation, players compete to see who can quickly score a set number of points. It's a fast-paced, heart-pounding version of the game that will test your reflexes and speed.

Table tennis is a versatile sport with exciting variations that cater to different tastes and skill levels. It's a pocket-sized version of tennis with a truckload of fun and excitement. Whether playing with friends or setting your sights on championship glory, ping pong offers a thrilling and speedy experience. Grab that paddle, find a partner, and get ready for some ping-tastic action on the table. It's all about high-speed high-fives and a whole lot of fun!

Chapter 2: Essential Equipment

The electrifying universe of table tennis is where speed meets strategy, where every split-second decision can be the difference between victory and defeat. As you venture deeper into the world of table tennis, you'll discover that beyond the dazzling rallies and spins, there's an essential toolkit that forms the backbone of this captivating sport. This chapter will unravel the secrets of the essential table tennis equipment. It's a tale of rackets, balls, and tables that will transform your game and elevate your passion for this dynamic sport to new heights.

Essential Table Tennis Equipment: The Game's Backbone

Success isn't solely dependent on your skills and techniques. The equipment you use plays a pivotal role in your performance. Whether you're a beginner or a seasoned pro, understanding the ins and outs of table tennis equipment is crucial for optimizing your ping pong experience.

The Table: The Centerpiece of the Game

3. *To play table tennis, you need a table. Source: https://unsplash.com/photos/man-in-white-t-shirt-and-blue-denim-jeans-sitting-on-green-grass-field-during-daytime-4P5SOGfnAOY?utm_content=creditShareLink&utm_medium=referral&utm_source=unsplash*

The table is where the magic happens. It's the game's centerpiece, setting the stage for thrilling rallies and strategic plays. Understanding the table's specifications and features is the first step in mastering this fast-paced sport.

- **Table Dimensions:** A standard table measures 9 feet in length, 5 feet in width, and stands 2.5 feet tall. It's divided into two halves by a net, and each side provides ample space for exciting gameplay. The table's dimensions are carefully regulated to ensure fairness in competition but can vary at home or in public spaces.

- **Table Surface:** The playing surface of a table tennis table is often made of high-quality wood, providing an excellent bounce for the ball. To facilitate fair gameplay, this surface should be smooth, level, and defect-free. The surface should be painted with a dark color, usually green or blue, to contrast with the ball.

- **Net and Posts:** The net divides the table into two halves and is held in place by net posts. The net should be 6 inches tall, with its bottom edge as close to the playing surface as possible. The tension of the net is crucial, ensuring that it doesn't sag or billow during play.

- **Legs and Support:** The table's legs and support system must be sturdy to stabilize during intense rallies. They should also be adjustable to ensure a level playing surface. Many high-quality tables feature a foldable design, making them convenient for storage and transport.

The table is where your table tennis journey begins and ends. Its dimensions, surface quality, and net design all contribute to the fairness and excitement of the game. Choosing the right table that meets your needs is the foundation of your ping-pong experience.

Rackets (Paddles): Your Weapon

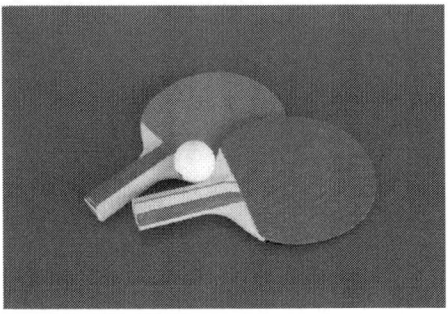

4. *Rackets are vital for playing table tennis. Source: https://unsplash.com/photos/blue-and-white-ball-and-white-golf-club-3B8nIiT-Pmc?utm_content=creditShareLink&utm_medium=referral&utm_source=unsplash*

The racket, also known as a paddle, is your weapon on the table tennis battlefield. It's the instrument through which you execute your shots, adding spin, speed, and control to the game. Understanding the key features of a table tennis racket is vital for making the right selection.

- **Blade:** The blade of a table tennis racket is the flat, wooden part that you hit the ball with. Blades are typically made of various layers of wood, varying in thickness and composition. Some blades include materials like carbon fiber for added power and stability. The choice of blade affects the racket's overall performance and feel.

- **Rubber:** The rubber covering on the blade's hitting surface plays a significant role in ball control and spin. There are two types of rubber—one with a pimpled surface (pips-out) and another with a smooth surface (pips-in). Players often use a combination of these rubbers on their rackets, with different colors (red and black) on each side to create varied spin and speed effects.

- **Sponge:** The rubber is attached to a sponge, and the thickness of this sponge affects the racket's performance. Thicker sponges provide more power and speed, while thinner ones offer more control. The sponge thickness choice is a matter of personal preference and playing style.

- **Handle:** The racket's handle comes in various shapes and sizes, allowing players to find a grip that suits their hand comfortably. The choice of handle can significantly impact your ability to maneuver the racket effectively.

Your table tennis racket is an extension of your playing style and preferences. The combination of blade, rubber, sponge, and handle makes it a personalized tool. Whether you seek power, control, or a balanced mix, understanding the components of your racket is essential for optimizing your game.

Balls: The Precise Sphere of Play

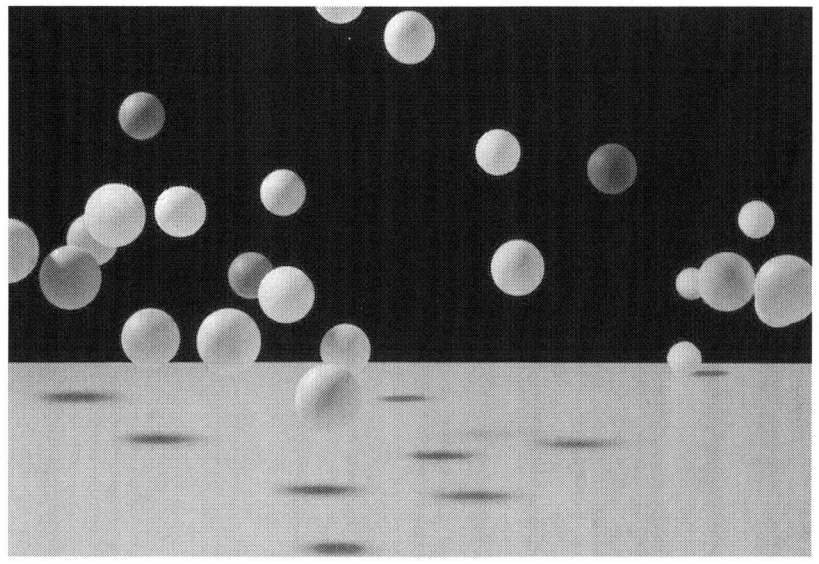

5. *Table tennis balls are designed to be lightweight. Source: https://unsplash.com/photos/assorted-color-bubbles-illustration-fIMqGvVaATk?utm_content=creditShareLink&utm_medium=referral&utm_source=unsplash*

The table tennis ball is a marvel of engineering, designed for precise bounce, spin, and speed. The tiny, lightweight sphere dances across the table, responding to every flick of the racket. Understanding the key attributes of table tennis balls is crucial for an exceptional playing experience.

- **Size:** Table tennis balls are remarkably small, with a standard diameter of about 40 mm. Their compact size demands precision and skill, making the game fast-paced and exhilarating.

- **Weight:** Table tennis balls are featherlight, usually weighing around 2.7 grams. Their minimal weight ensures rapid movement and incredible spin potential. Lightweight balls are crucial for maintaining the agility and excitement of the game.

- **Material:** Table tennis balls are typically made of celluloid or plastic. While celluloid balls were prevalent in the past, plastic balls have become the standard due to environmental concerns and durability. The material of the ball affects the bounce and spin characteristics.

- **Color:** The color of table tennis balls varies between white and orange, although white is the standard color used in most official competitions. The choice of color can affect visibility and contrast against the playing surface.

The table tennis ball may be small, but it's a pivotal part of the game. Its size, weight, material, and color influence play dynamics, making every rally a unique and engaging challenge.

Safety and Additional Accessories

- **Safety Precautions:** Safety in table tennis is paramount. Players should ensure that the playing area is free from hazards and wear appropriate footwear to prevent slipping during intense rallies. Safety barriers and proper lighting should be in place for competitive play.

- **Additional Accessories:** Besides the core equipment, players may use accessories such as racket cases, which protect their paddles, or table tennis robot machines for solo practice. These accessories can enhance the overall playing experience and convenience.

Table tennis is a sport that hinges on the quality of the equipment you use. From the table to the racket and the ball, each component contributes to the excitement and precision of the game. Understanding the intricacies of these essential items empowers players to make informed choices, ensuring they're equipped for thrilling table tennis experiences.

Setting up Your Ultimate Table Tennis Space

Set up your table tennis space before you start smashing that ping pong ball. Whether you have a spacious game room, a cozy living room, or an outdoor area, creating the right environment is crucial for an unforgettable ping pong experience.

Table Selection: Finding the Perfect Ping Pong Platform

Kick off your ping pong adventure with the star of the show, the table. Choosing the right one is a game-changer for your ping-pong sessions. If you're looking for a more authentic and competitive experience, invest in a standard-sized table recognized by the International Table Tennis Federation (ITTF). However, for casual players and those short on space, there are compact, foldable tables available. Some even have wheels, making them easy to move around.

Pro Tip 1: Measure your space carefully before buying a table to ensure it fits comfortably and allows players to move freely during the game.

Pro Tip 2: Opt for a table with adjustable legs if your floor isn't perfectly level. It'll save you from unsafe games.

Room Layout: The Ping Pong Dance Floor

Now that you've got your table, it's time to find the perfect spot for it. If you're lucky enough to have a dedicated game room, you can go all out with your ping-pong decor. Think neon lights, ping pong-themed posters, and perhaps even a mini-fridge stocked with refreshments. It's all about creating an awesome hangout space for your friends and family.

The living room can double as your ping-pong playground for those with more limited space. You can easily move some furniture to make room for your table, but first, move any breakable items to a safe place before the game begins. Create a layout that allows for comfortable movement around the table, ensuring everyone can join the fun.

Pro Tip: Invest in furniture sliders to protect your floors from scratches and dents when moving furniture for a game. They'll make the process smoother and safer.

Lighting: Shedding Light on the Game

Ping pong is all about fast reflexes, and proper lighting is essential to avoid shadows and ensure that the ball is easy to track. Opt for bright, even lighting that covers the entire playing area. Overhead lighting or adjustable LED lamps are excellent choices. These ensure good visibility and add to the overall ambiance of your ping-pong arena.

Pro Tip 1: If you want a more relaxed atmosphere, consider adding dimmable lighting. It will set the mood and make your space versatile for different occasions.

Pro Tip 2: To create an immersive environment, you can install color-changing LED lights around your ping pong area. It will provide the necessary illumination and add a fun, dynamic touch to your space.

Flooring: A Firm Foundation

Having the right flooring beneath your ping-pong table can make a world of difference in overall gameplay. If you're setting up your table outdoors, ensure a hard, level surface, like a concrete patio. Grass or uneven ground can be a real buzzkill for your game.

Pro Tip: If you're concerned about your indoor flooring getting scratched, consider investing in ping-pong floor protectors. They're like little shoes for your table's legs, preventing floor damage.

Wall Décor: Amp up the Atmosphere

Why not add wall decor to create a true ping-pong palace? You can hang ping pong artwork, posters of your favorite players, or even create a wall of fame to document epic matches with friends and family. The key is to infuse your space with a sense of fun and competition. It's not just a game but an experience!

Storage Solutions: Declutter with Panache

Ping-pong equipment can take up space, especially if you're an avid player. Consider investing in stylish storage solutions to keep your space tidy and organized. Ping-pong tables with built-in storage are a fantastic option, as they have dedicated compartments to stow away your gear, like extra balls and rackets. If you're going the DIY route, some sleek shelving or a dedicated ping-pong cart will keep things organized and at arm's reach.

Pro Tip 1: Label your storage containers or shelves to ensure quick and easy access to your ping pong gear. There's nothing worse than frantically searching for a missing ball when a game is heating up.

Pro Tip 2: Use the storage area as an opportunity to add a touch of personal style. Use colorful bins, decorative baskets, or adhesive hooks for your rackets.

Entertainment System: Turn up the Ping Pong Playlist

While the thrill of the game is entertaining enough, a little music can add some extra pep to your space. Create a ping pong playlist with your favorite tunes, whether upbeat pop hits, classic rock anthems, or some funky beats. Music sets the mood and will keep you and your guests grooving between rallies. Plus, depending on your mood, it's an excellent way to get into the competitive spirit or keep things light and fun.

Pro Tip 1: Consider investing in a mini speaker system if you're a ping pong enthusiast. The right sound system will make your ping-pong space feel like a real party.

Pro Tip 2: To add an extra layer of fun, have a mini dance-off between games. It's a great way to keep everyone entertained and the energy levels high.

Personalize Your Ping Pong Space: Make It Yours

Lastly, personalize your ping pong space to make it uniquely yours. Let your personality shine through, whether it's a wall of fame, a quirky poster, or a gallery of action shots. Your ping pong space should reflect your love for the game and create an inviting atmosphere for friends and family. It's not just about the game but the unforgettable moments you'll create in this space.

Pro Tip: Involve your friends and family in the decorating process. It's fun to bond, share your passion for ping pong, and get them excited about future games and gatherings.

Setting up your ping pong space is a creative and exciting endeavor. Whether you have a whole game room to transform, a living room to adapt, or an outdoor area to conquer, your ping-pong paradise awaits. With the right table, lighting, decor, and a personalized touch, you can create an atmosphere perfect for epic ping pong matches and unforgettable moments with friends and family. So, gather your gear, queue up the ping pong playlist, and let the games begin.

Chapter 3: Grips and Strokes

As you strive to become a ping pong pro, there are two fundamental pillars you must master. Grips and strokes are the essence of your ping pong prowess, determining how you handle your paddle and send the ball zipping across the table. In this chapter, you'll dive deep into the captivating art of grips and strokes, unlocking the secrets that will elevate your table tennis game.

Grips and strokes are the heartbeat of table tennis. They are your tools for creating thrilling rallies, generating wicked spins, and outmaneuvering your opponents. In ping pong, understanding the intricacies of grips and strokes is your key to unlocking a treasure trove of skills and strategies. So, prepare to immerse yourself in the fascinating world of grips and strokes, where precision, agility, and creativity combine to form the foundation of your table tennis expertise.

Mastering the Art of Racket Grips and Techniques

Table tennis starts with that little piece of equipment in your hand, the racket. It's time for you to explore racket grips and techniques in table tennis. Whether you're a beginner eager to learn the basics or an advanced player looking to fine-tune your skills, here's what you need to know.

The Basics of Racket Grips

Before diving into the intricate techniques of table tennis, it's essential to understand the fundamentals of racket grips. How you hold your racket will significantly impact your control, power, and spin. Table tennis has two primary grips: the shakehand and the penhold grip.

1. **Shakehand Grip:** The shakehand grip is one of the most common and versatile grips in table tennis. To achieve this grip:

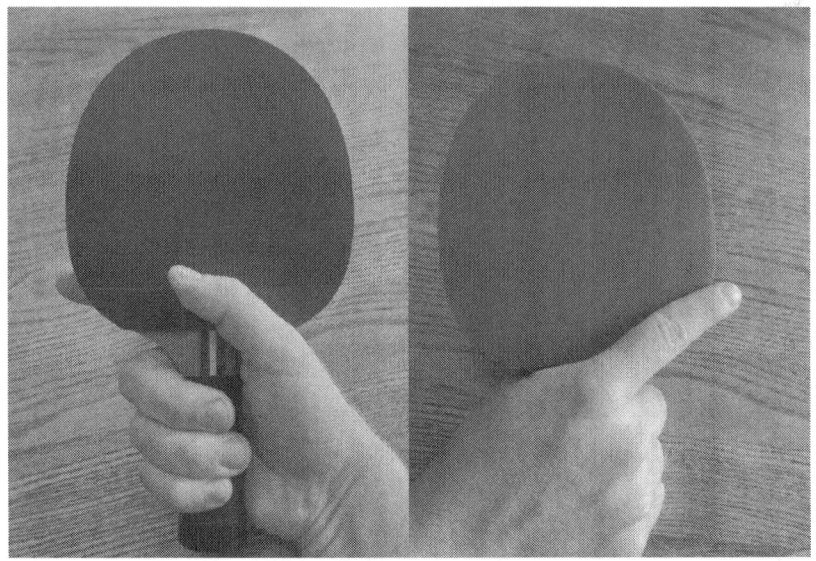

6. *The shakehand grip. Source: Leanmeangreenbeanmachine, CC BY-SA 4.0 <https://creativecommons.org/licenses/by-sa/4.0>, via Wikimedia Commons: https://commons.wikimedia.org/wiki/File:Shakehand_fh_bh.png*

1. Hold the racket as if you are offering a handshake.

2. Place your thumb on the backhand side of the blade, with your index finger resting on the other side.

3. Wrap your other three fingers around the handle.

4. The blade should be perpendicular to your hand, with the rubber facing the opponent.

The shakehand grip provides good control and flexibility, making it suitable for various playing styles. It allows for both backhand and forehand shots with ease.

2. **Penhold Grip:** The penhold grip gets its name from how the racket handle is held, resembling how one holds a pen. To achieve this grip:

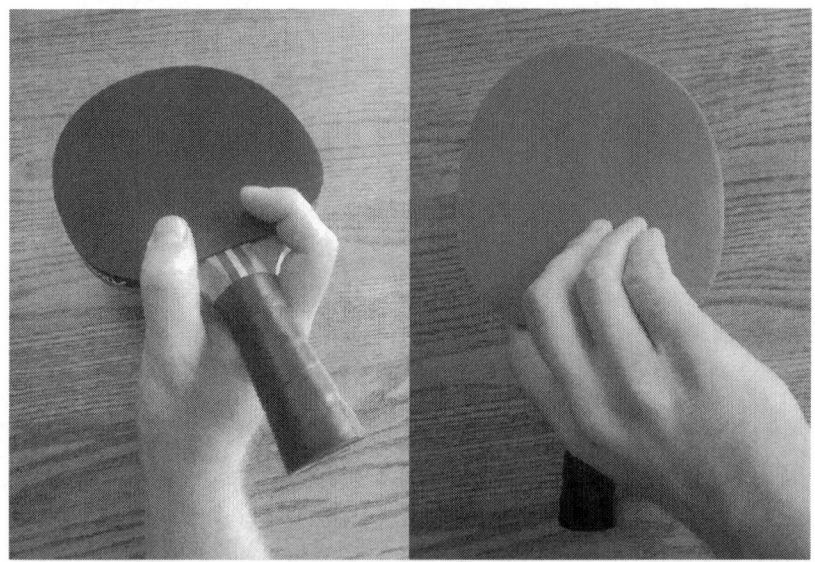

7. *The penhold grip. Source: Leanmeangreenbeanmachine, CC BY-SA 4.0 <https://creativecommons.org/licenses/by-sa/4.0>, via Wikimedia Commons: https://commons.wikimedia.org/wiki/File:Cpen_fh_bh.png*

1. Use your thumb and index finger to hold the racket handle, much like a pen.

2. Your thumb should be on the backhand side of the blade, while your index finger is on the forehand side.

3. The other three fingers are usually tucked against the handle for stability.

The penhold grip is known for its close-to-the-table gameplay and swift wrist action. It's popular in Asian countries and is ideal for players who excel in quick, close-to-the-net shots.

Grip Size: The size of the racket handle can vary, so it's crucial to choose one that feels comfortable in your hand. A handle that's too small might result in a lack of control, while a handle that's too large can hinder your wrist movement. Experiment with different grip sizes to find the most comfortable one for your playing style.

Fundamental Table Tennis Techniques

Now that you've got a grip (pun intended) on the basics, it's time to explore the fundamental techniques of table tennis. These building blocks will elevate your game, regardless of your skill level.

1. **The Serve:** The serve is your introduction to every point in table tennis. It's a strategic element that can catch your opponent off guard and set the tone for the rally. Some key aspects of a good serve include:

8. *Serve techniques. Source:*
https://www.researchgate.net/publication/325510301/figure/fig1/ AS:632770497871874@1527875651796/Four-key-events-between- squat-and-standing-serves-in-table-tennis-Full-size-DOI.png

- **Variety:** Mix up your serves with different spins (backspin, sidespin, topspin) and placement to keep your opponent guessing.

- **Placement:** Aim for areas on the table that exploit your opponent's weaknesses.

- **Consistency:** Develop services that you can execute reliably under pressure.

2. **The Forehand Loop:** The forehand loop is a dynamic offensive cornerstone of table tennis. It involves generating topspin by brushing the ball, creating a curved trajectory that lands on your opponent's side of the table, making it harder to return due to the extra speed. To master the forehand loop:

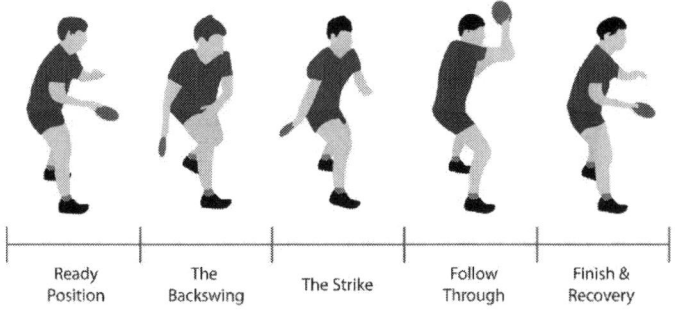

9. *The forehand loop technique. Source: https://static.wixstatic.com/media/080888_88168e009c314119a6 0e5f93447187b7~mv2.png/v1/fill/w_640,h_304,al_c,q_85,usm_0. 66_1.00_0.01,enc_auto/080888_88168e009c314119a60e5f934471 87b7~mv2.png*

- **Footwork:** Position yourself well to get into a balanced stance.

- **Body Rotation:** Rotate your body, transferring weight from the back leg to the front leg.

- **Timing:** Make contact with the ball at the peak of its bounce.

- **Follow Through:** Swing your arm forward upward for maximum topspin.

3. **The Backhand Counter:** The backhand counter is a defensive shot used to effectively return an opponent's shots. It's about maintaining control and accuracy. Key points to remember for a solid backhand counter are:

READY POSITION BACKSWING STRIKING THE BALL FOLLOW THROUGH AND RECOVER

10. Backhand counter technique. Source: https://racketinsight.com/wp-content/uploads/2021/07/How-to-Play-a-Backhand-Drive-1024x512.jpg.webp

- **Balance:** Stay balanced with your weight slightly forward.

- **Grip:** Adjust your grip to facilitate quick and controlled wrist movement.

- **Timing:** Make contact with the ball early to ensure a clean return.

- **Consistency:** Develop a consistent backhand counter to rely on during matches.

1. **Footwork:** Footwork is the foundation of table tennis. It allows you to position yourself correctly for every shot, react swiftly, and maintain balance during rallies. Some footwork principles include:

- **Ready Position:** Always be prepared to move by keeping your knees bent and weight on the balls of your feet.

- **Small Steps:** Use small, quick steps to adjust your positioning.

- **Anticipation:** Read your opponent's shots and position yourself accordingly.

1. **Spin Control:** Table tennis is all about spin. Learning to read and respond to the spin on the ball is crucial for success. You can practice spin control by:

- **Watching the Ball:** Focus on the ball's rotation as it approaches your racket.

- **Adjusting Your Racket Angle:** Tilt your racket to match the spin of the incoming ball.

- **Practice with Different Spin Variations:** Work with practice partners to understand and handle various spins.

Advanced Techniques

As you progress in your table tennis journey, you may want to explore more advanced techniques:

1. **The Smash:** The smash is a powerful offensive shot that can end a point in an instant. To execute a successful smash, you need:

- **A High Ball:** The ball should be high above the net for a proper smash.

- **Timing:** Time your shot so that you make contact at the highest point of the ball's trajectory.

- **Power and Precision:** Use your entire body to generate power and direct the ball effectively.

2. **The Chop:** The chop is a defensive shot that imparts a heavy backspin on the ball. It's typically used when the ball is low and spinning strongly. The keys to a successful chop include:

- **A Low Crouch:** Get low to the table to prepare for the shot.

- **Smooth Stroke:** Maintain a smooth and controlled stroke to impart backspin.

- **Contact Point:** Contact the ball on its lower portion to maximize backspin.

1. **The Lob:** The lob is an effective defensive shot that sends the ball high and deep into your opponent's side of the table. To execute a good lob:

- **Distance from the Table:** Position yourself away from the table to allow for a high arc.

- **Racket Angle:** Tilt your racket to control the trajectory and spin.

- **Anticipation:** Read your opponent's positioning and shots to determine when a lob is necessary.

Drills and Practice

The key to mastering table tennis techniques is practice. Consider engaging in specific drills to hone your skills. These drills can focus on footwork, serve and return, or a particular shot like the forehand loop. Practicing with a partner or a coach can also provide valuable feedback to help you improve. Recording your practice sessions on video can be beneficial for analyzing and refining your technique.

Table tennis is a sport that rewards technique, strategy, and practice. Whether you're a beginner looking to establish a strong foundation or an advanced player striving to perfect your game, mastering racket grips and techniques is a journey worth undertaking. With the right grip, a solid understanding of the fundamentals, and a commitment to practice, you'll be well on your way to becoming a formidable table tennis player.

Unveiling Forehand and Backhand Strokes

Table tennis, a sport of lightning-fast rallies and precision, is driven by the art of strokes. The forehand and backhand strokes form the foundation of every player's arsenal among the myriad of shots.

The Importance of Stroke Techniques

Stroke techniques in table tennis are akin to brush strokes on a canvas, each one contributing to the masterpiece that is your game. Your ability to execute forehand and backhand strokes efficiently and consistently can determine the outcome of a match. Understanding the nuances of these strokes will empower you to dictate the game's flow, dominate your opponent, and elevate your play to the next level.

Forehand Stroke: Unleashing the Power

11. The forehand stroke. Source: https://racketinsight.com/wp-content/uploads/2021/07/How-to-Play-a-Forehand-Drive-1024x512.jpg

The forehand stroke, often hailed as the weapon of choice in table tennis, is the foundation of offensive play. It's characterized by its ability to deliver power, spin, and precision in a single motion. Here's how to perfect your forehand:

1. Stance and Positioning

1. Start with a balanced stance with your feet shoulder-width apart.

2. Position your body sideways to the table with your non-dominant foot forward.

3. Bend your knees slightly, keeping your weight on the balls of your feet.

4. Maintain an upright posture with your torso rotated to face the net.

2. Grip

1. For the forehand stroke, the shakehand grip is ideal.

2. The racket handle should rest in your palm, and your fingers should wrap around it firmly but comfortably.

3. Keep your thumb on the backhand side of the racket and your fingers on the forehand side.

3. Swing Mechanics

1. Start the swing by pivoting at your hips and rotating your torso.

2. Keep your non-dominant hand out in front for balance and better control.

3. As the ball approaches, draw your racket back behind you.

4. For topspin, brush the ball upward and forward, generating spin and speed.

5. Follow through with your racket, finishing above your shoulder on the same side.

4. Footwork

   1. Move your feet to position yourself optimally for the shot.

   2. Adjust your stance as you shift between forehand and backhand strokes.

   3. Return to the ready position after each stroke.

5. Timing

   1. Make contact with the ball at the peak of its bounce to maximize control and spin.

   2. Adjust your racket's timing and angle to adapt to different types of shots and spins.

The forehand stroke is a versatile weapon that allows you to unleash powerful topspin, drive shots, and control placement. To become proficient, practice is key. Engage in forehand-specific drills and gradually increase the complexity of the shots you face. Experiment with variations of the forehand stroke, such as the forehand loop or flick, to add diversity to your game.

Backhand Stroke: The Defensive Anchor

While the forehand is the go-to offensive stroke, the backhand is your defensive stronghold. It enables you to return the fastest and most powerful shots with control, accuracy, and finesse. Here's how to perfect your backhand:

1. Stance and Positioning

   1. Adopt a similar balanced stance to the forehand shot, with your feet shoulder-width apart.

2. Position your body sideways to the table, with your dominant foot forward.

3. Slightly bend your knees, maintaining your weight on the balls of your feet.

4. Keep your torso upright and rotate it to face the net.

2. Grip

1. The shakehand grip is also suitable for the backhand stroke.

2. Hold the racket handle securely but comfortably in your palm.

3. Position your thumb on the backhand side and your fingers on the forehand side.

3. Swing Mechanics

1. Start the swing by rotating your hips and torso, similar to the forehand.

2. Keep your non-dominant hand in front for balance.

3. Draw the racket back behind you as the ball approaches.

4. For topspin, brush the ball in a forward and upward motion.

5. Finish the stroke with your racket in front of you, at about eye level.

4. Footwork

1. Move your feet to position yourself optimally for the backhand shot.

2. Adjust your stance when transitioning between forehand and backhand strokes.

3. Return to the ready position after executing the stroke.

5. Timing

1. Make contact with the ball at the peak of its bounce to maintain control and spin.

2. Adapt your timing and racket angle to respond to different spins and shot types.

The backhand stroke is reliable for returning shots with precision, controlling rallies, and defending opponents' attacks. To master it, dedicate time to backhand-focused drills, including the return of serve and blocking exercises. Develop a strong backhand flick to counter short balls and surprise your opponents with a sudden offensive move.

Practicing Forehand and Backhand Strokes

Effective practice is the key to honing your stroke techniques in table tennis. Here are some strategies to help you improve:

1. Drills

- Engage in structured drills that focus on forehand and backhand strokes.

- Include consistency drills, in which you practice delivering controlled shots repetitively.

- Mix in live ball drills, where you perform specific scenarios against a practice partner.

- Dedicate sessions to perfecting the forehand or backhand strokes separately.

2. Video Analysis

- Record your practice sessions on video to analyze your technique.

- Review your videos to identify areas for improvement in your footwork, timing, and swing mechanics.
- Seek feedback from coaches or experienced players based on your video analysis.

3. Game Play

- Participate in practice matches to apply your stroke techniques in real-game situations.
- Experiment with different shot combinations and strategies to enhance your versatility.
- Play against opponents of varying skill levels to adapt to different playing styles.

4. Consistency and Repetition

- Focus on consistency and repetition in your practice.
- Develop muscle memory by consistently executing forehand and backhand strokes with precision.
- Gradually increase the complexity of the shots you face during practice.

5. Mental Training

- Work on the mental aspects of your game, including focus, concentration, and decision-making.
- Practice visualization techniques to envision successful stroke execution and improve your shot selection.

Developing a Winning Mindset

Beyond the physical and technical aspects of stroke techniques, developing a winning mindset is essential in table tennis. Here are some mental aspects to consider:

- **Confidence:** Build your confidence by practicing regularly and developing a strong foundation in your stroke techniques. Believe in your ability to execute your shots with precision and consistency.

- **Adaptability:** Be adaptable and willing to adjust your strategies based on your opponent's playing style. Make quick decisions during rallies, choosing the most appropriate stroke for each situation.
- **Mental Toughness:** Develop mental toughness to remain composed under pressure. Embrace challenges and view them as opportunities to grow and improve.
- **Focus and Concentration:** Train your mind to maintain unwavering focus and concentration during matches. Stay in the present moment and concentrate on executing each stroke with precision.

Mastering the art of forehand and backhand strokes in table tennis is a journey that requires dedication, practice, and the development of a strong foundation. With the proper grip, stance, and swing mechanics, you can become a formidable player capable of delivering powerful offensive forehand strokes and reliable defensive backhand strokes.

The art of grip and stroke techniques is not merely about physical execution but also about developing a winning mindset that fosters confidence, adaptability, mental toughness, focus, and concentration. So, pick up your racket, hit the table, and embark on mastering forehand and backhand strokes in the thrilling world of table tennis.

Chapter 4: Serving and Receiving

In the vast universe of table tennis, the serve is not merely the initiation of a rally. It's a strategic masterpiece, a moment of intense focus and skill. Similarly, receiving serves is not about hitting the ball back but reading your opponent, predicting the spin, and executing the perfect return. In this chapter, you'll unravel the secrets of serving and receiving in table tennis. From mastering diverse serving techniques to formulating strategies for impeccable returns, you'll be equipped with the knowledge and skills to elevate your game.

The Art of the Serve: Crafting Your Opening Move

12. Serving effectively can determine the outcome of the match. Source: Mohan Doha Stadium Plus Qatar, CC BY 2.0 <https://creativecommons.org/licenses/by/2.0>, via Wikimedia Commons: https://commons.wikimedia.org/wiki/File:Ma_Lin_OQ_2012.jpg

The serve is your canvas, and the ball is your brush. Just as a painter starts a masterpiece with a single stroke, a table tennis match begins with a serve. Your ability to serve effectively and receive strategically can determine the outcome of a match. In this section, you'll explore the essential elements of a great serve, the types you can master, and the strategic considerations that make your serve a powerful weapon on the table tennis battlefield.

Understanding the Basics

Before you dive into advanced serving techniques, it's crucial to establish a firm foundation with the basic principles of a good serve. A successful serve encompasses the following elements:

- **Ball Placement:** Precision is key. Aim for specific spots on the opponent's side of the table to exploit their weaknesses.

- **Spin Variation:** Master different spins, such as topspin, backspin, and sidespin, to keep your opponent guessing.

- **Deception:** Use subtle movements and body language to conceal your intended spin and placement until the last moment.

- **Consistency:** Develop services that you can execute consistently. A reliable service forms the basis for more complex variations.

A successful serve is a calculated move that sets the tone for the rally. By understanding the core principles of serving, you can build a strong foundation for mastering this crucial game aspect.

Types of Serves

Serving is not a one-size-fits-all affair. There are different types of serves to add diversity and unpredictability to your game.

- **Forehand Pendulum Serve:** A deceptive serve where the racket swings like a pendulum, generating sidespin and topspin.

- **Backhand Tomahawk Serve:** An aggressive serve with sidespin, executed with a chopping motion.

- **Reverse Pendulum Serve:** A spinny serve with varying amounts of sidespin and backspin, confusing opponents with its unpredictable bounce.

- **Ghost Serve:** A serve with no spin, making it challenging for the opponent to read the ball's trajectory.

The ability to serve with different spins and placements can catch your opponent off guard and set you up for the next move. Mastering these various serve types will give you a tactical advantage.

Strategic Serving

Serving is about setting up the point and keeping your opponent on their toes. Here are the strategic aspects of serving that you must keep in mind:

- **Setting up the Point:** Use your serve to set up the next shot. Plan your serve to lead to a favorable third-shot attack (the shot after your opponent returns the ball).

- **Targeting Weaknesses:** Analyze your opponent's weaknesses and serve to exploit them. If they struggle with backhand returns, focus your serves in that area.

- **Changing the Pace:** Vary the speed of your serves. Mix fast, long serves with slower, short serves to keep opponents off balance.

- **Long and Fast Serve:** A serve deep and fast to the corners of the table can catch opponents off guard, setting you up for an aggressive follow-up shot.

Serving requires you to set up your next move strategically. You will gain a significant advantage in your matches by understanding the tactical aspects of serving.

Serve and Attack Drills

Practice is the key to perfecting your serving skills. It's time to explore specific drills to refine your serve and transition seamlessly into offensive shots.

- **Serve and Loop Drill:** Practice serving followed by strong forehand loops. This drill improves your ability to transition from serve to attack seamlessly.

- **Serve and Backhand Flick Drill:** Work on serves followed by quick backhand flicks. This drill enhances your backhand response to short serves.

Drills are the bridge between theory and mastery. Engaging in specific serve and attack drills will help you refine your skills and adapt your serves to different playing situations.

Strategies for Receiving Serves: Decoding Your Opponent

Receiving a serve is an opportunity to turn the tables in your favor. Here's an exploration of the art of reading your opponent's serves, effective receiving techniques, and strategies for successful receives.

Reading the Spin

Reading the spin on the ball is the first step to an effective return. There are two main techniques to decode your opponent's serve:

- **Watching the Contact:** Focus on your opponent's racket to observe their contact with the ball. The angle and motion of their racket indicate the spin.

- **Ball Trajectory:** Observe the ball's trajectory after it bounces on the opponent's side. The curve and bounce can reveal the spin type.

Reading the spin on the ball is a critical skill in table tennis. By observing your opponent's racket and the ball's trajectory, you can anticipate and respond effectively to different spins.

Effective Receiving Techniques

Effective receiving goes beyond merely getting the ball over the net. Here are a few techniques for receiving services.

- **Forehand Push:** A controlled, low-impact shot to return backspin serves. Angle the racket slightly downward and use a smooth stroke to return the ball short over the net.

- **Backhand Flick:** A quick, aggressive shot against short serves. Use your wrist to generate speed and flick the ball over the net with topspin.

- **Forehand Flip:** A powerful shot against high and slightly long serves. Step in, meet the ball at its peak, and use quick wrist action to hit it aggressively.

Effective receiving techniques allow you to return serves precisely and set yourself up for the next move. By mastering these techniques, you can control the pace of the rally.

Strategic Receives

Receiving serves is not a passive act but an opportunity to seize control of the rally. It's time to explore strategies for successful receives.

- **Short and Low Returns:** Keep your returns short and low over the net to deny your opponent the opportunity for aggressive attacks.

- **Flick to Wide Angles:** Use flicks and aggressive returns to exploit wide angles, forcing your opponent out of position.

- **Varying Returns:** Change your receive strategy throughout the match. Avoid predictability by mixing short, long, aggressive, and passive returns.

Strategic receives can disrupt your opponent's game and create opportunities for counterattacks. You can gain the upper hand in a rally by varying your returns and targeting specific areas.

Anticipating Serves

Anticipating your opponent's serves is a skill that can give you an edge. Here are two techniques to predict your opponent's serves:

- **Recognizing Patterns:** Experienced players often have serving patterns. Analyze your opponent's previous serves to anticipate their next move.

- **Quick Decision Making:** Make split-second decisions based on your opponent's serve. Train your reflexes to respond effectively to varying spins and speeds.

Anticipating your opponent's serves and making quick decisions is a skill that can turn defense into offense. By reading patterns and reacting swiftly, you gain a tactical advantage.

Receiving and Counterattacking Drills

Practice makes perfect, and that holds for receiving serves. Here are two drills to refine your receiving skills and immediately follow up with counterattacks:

- **Random Serve Drill:** Have a practice partner serve randomly with different spins and lengths. Focus on adapting your receives accordingly.

- **Receive and Counter Drill:** Practice receiving serves and immediately follow up with an attack. This drill enhances your ability to transition from defense to offense.

Drills that focus on receiving and counterattacking are invaluable for game scenarios. You will become more versatile and flexible in your matches by practicing these drills.

Serving and receiving are not just technical aspects of table tennis. They are strategic tools that can tip the balance of a match in your favor. By mastering the art of the serve, you dictate the pace of the game, forcing your opponent to dance to your rhythm. Similarly, good receiving techniques allow you to read your opponent's moves, respond effectively, and turn their serves into counterattack opportunities.

Remember, practice, adaptability, and keen observation are your allies in perfecting these skills. You can transform your serving and receiving abilities into powerful weapons on the table tennis battlefield through consistent practice, drills, and a deep understanding of your opponent's game. So, pick up your racket, visualize your opponent's moves, and let the artistry of serving and receiving propel you to victory. May your serves be sharp, your receives be precise, and your victories be abundant.

Chapter 5: Singles Play

In the world of table tennis, nothing epitomizes the essence of individual mastery quite like a singles match. It's a symphony of skill, strategy, and mental fortitude where every stroke, every serve, and every movement matter. In this chapter, you'll dive into the heart of single play in table tennis. You'll discover the rules, strategies, and the art of developing your singles game. Whether you're a newcomer looking to step onto the singles stage or a seasoned player aiming to elevate your solo performance, this chapter has something for everyone.

Singles Game Rules and Strategies

13. *A singles game is one that involves you and one opponent. Source: https://unsplash.com/photos/man-in-orange-t-shirt-sitting-on-chair-XpLWpyrAbAo?utm_content=creditShareLink&utm_medium=referral&utm_source=unsplash*

A singles match in table tennis is like a chess game of rapid exchanges and lightning-quick moves. Understanding the rules and having a strategic game plan are essential. It's time to discover the rules and strategies to make you a formidable singles player.

Understanding Singles Game Rules

Before you step onto the singles stage, it's crucial to understand the rules that govern the game. Here's a concise breakdown of the key rules:

- **Scoring:** Matches are usually played to 11 points, and the player or pair who reaches 11 points first with a margin of at least two points wins the game.

- **Serving:** In singles, the server alternates sides every two points. The ball must bounce on both the server's and receiver's sides.

- **Serve Rotation:** The receiver can choose which side to receive the serve. However, the choice must be maintained for the entire game.

- **Let Service:** If the ball hits the net but still goes over, it's called a "let," and the serve is retaken. There's no limit on the number of "lets" during service.

- **Change of Ends:** Players switch sides when an odd number of games have been played—after the first game and every two games thereafter.

- **Tie-Break:** If the score reaches 10-10, a player must win by two points. This is often referred to as "deuce."

A successful singles match is about understanding the rules, adapting to the nuances of service rotation, and maintaining a sharp focus throughout the game.

Singles Strategies for Success

Now, it's time to explore the strategic aspects of playing singles. Developing a game plan and understanding your opponent's style are keys to victory.

- **Adaptability:** Adjust your game according to your opponent's strengths and weaknesses. Your strategy may need to change during the match.

- **Serve Variation:** Experiment with different types of serves to keep your opponent guessing. Vary the placement, spin, and speed.

- **Effective Footwork:** Footwork is critical in singles. Move efficiently to position yourself for the best possible shot.

- **Control the Table:** Aim to control the center of the table and dictate the rally. This strategic placement can limit your opponent's options.

- **Mix Defense and Offense:** Be ready to switch between defensive and offensive play as the situation demands. Sometimes, a well-placed block can be as effective as a powerful attack.

Successful singles strategies involve a blend of adaptability, smart serving, efficient footwork, table control, and a balanced mix of offense and defense. Mastering these elements will give you a significant advantage over your opponent.

Developing Your Singles Game

Your journey as a singles player doesn't end with rule knowledge and a basic strategy. You must focus on honing your skills and creating a personalized playing style to excel.

Technical Proficiency

Technical proficiency is the backbone of your singles game. Mastering the fundamental techniques will provide a solid foundation for your singles performance.

- **Forehand and Backhand Drives:** Ensure your drives are powerful, consistent, and well-placed. Practice different variations to keep your opponent guessing.

- **Serve and Receive Skills:** Perfect your serving techniques and develop your ability to read and return serves. A strong serve can set the tone of the match, while effective receiving can disrupt your opponent's rhythm.

- **Footwork:** Develop agile footwork to cover the table effectively and position yourself for the best shots. Footwork drills significantly enhance your ability to move swiftly and maintain balance.

- **Blocking and Counterattacking:** Practice your blocking skills to neutralize your opponent's attacks, and work on counterattacking techniques to seize the advantage when your opponent is off-balance.

Technical proficiency is your ticket to success in singles. Regular practice, guidance from a coach, and a keen eye for detail are essential in refining your techniques.

Creating a Personalized Playing Style

Each player has a unique style. Creating your personalized style involves honing your strengths and minimizing your weaknesses.

- **Offensive Player:** If you enjoy attacking, develop powerful forehand and backhand shots and create opportunities to unleash your offensive game. Incorporate loops, smashes, and drives into your offensive repertoire.

- **Defensive Player:** If defense is your forte, concentrate on your blocking and chopping skills. Develop the ability to return even the most aggressive shots with control. Learn different defensive strokes like chops, floats, and lobs to vary your game.

- **All-Round Player:** If you aim to be well-rounded, strive to balance your offensive and defensive skills. Adapt your style based on the strengths and weaknesses of your opponents. Develop a reliable backhand to complement your forehand attacks.

Your playing style defines your identity as a player. Embrace your natural inclinations, refine your strengths, and work on minimizing your weaknesses to create a style that suits your personality and capabilities.

Mental Resilience

The singles game can be mentally demanding. Develop mental resilience to stay focused and composed during the match.

- **Concentration:** Train your mind to maintain unwavering attention throughout the match. Stay in the moment and focus on each point. Mental imagery and mindfulness techniques can enhance your concentration.

- **Adaptability:** Be prepared to adjust your strategy and style as the match progresses. A flexible mindset is crucial in singles. Practice scenarios where you intentionally change your tactics to adapt to different game situations.

- **Confidence:** Believe in your skills and your game plan. Confidence is the difference between victory and defeat. Positive self-talk and visualization exercises can boost your confidence levels.

Mental resilience is the glue that holds your game together. Cultivate a strong mental game through meditation, visualization, and positive affirmations to keep your composure in high-pressure situations.

Training and Practice

Consistent training and practice are essential for your growth as a singles player. Engage in various drills and exercises to improve your skills, such as:

- **Serve and Receive Drills:** Practice various serve and receive scenarios to enhance your ability to adapt to different playing styles. Simulate game situations by mimicking various serve placements, spins, and speeds.

- **Match Simulations:** Play practice matches to simulate game situations and develop your competitive edge. Playing against opponents with varying styles will help you adapt quickly during actual matches.

- **Footwork Drills:** Specific footwork exercises can help you move efficiently and position your body for the best shots. Exercises like ladder drills, side shuffles, and diagonal movements can improve your agility.

- **Mental Training:** Work on meditation and stress management to strengthen your mental game. Practice mindful breathing and visualization of match scenarios to build mental resilience.

Training and practice are the engines that drive your improvement as a singles player. Seek guidance from experienced coaches, incorporate a variety of drills into your practice routine, and continuously push the boundaries of your skills.

The world of singles in table tennis is a unique and exhilarating experience. It's a canvas to paint your style, strategy, and character. Understanding the rules and crafting a game plan is just the beginning. Your journey as a singles player involves continuous development, adaptation, and growth.

Whether you're aiming for a local tournament or simply looking to improve your solo performance, the knowledge and skills you've acquired here will be your companions on this captivating journey. May your singles symphony resonate with precision, strategy, and the sweet sound of victory.

Chapter 6: Doubles Play

Like any art form, table tennis becomes more enchanting when shared. In the world of doubles play, the rhythm of the game changes as partnerships are forged, strategies are synchronized, and teamwork takes center stage. In this chapter, you'll navigate the unique aspects of doubles table tennis, from the rules that shape the game to the harmony of team dynamics and the strategies that will lead you to success. Whether you're preparing for a friendly match or have your sights set on competitive play, this chapter holds the key to becoming a formidable doubles player.

Doubles Rules and Team Dynamics

14. A doubles game involves a synchronized performance with your teammate. Source: Marcus Cyron, CC BY-SA 3.0 <https://creativecommons.org/licenses/by-sa/3.0>, via Wikimedia Commons: https://commons.wikimedia.org/wiki/File:Table_tennis_at_the_2 018_Summer_Youth_Olympics_%E2%80%93_Mixed_Final_Doub les_165.jpg

Doubles play in table tennis is not merely about sharing the table with a partner. It's a synchronized performance where teamwork, strategy, and understanding your partner's moves are crucial. It's time to explore the rules and team dynamics that make doubles a distinctive and captivating facet of the game.

Understanding Doubles Game Rules

Before you step into the complexities of team dynamics and strategy, you must lay the foundation with a clear understanding of the rules that govern doubles play. In a doubles match, the rules differ slightly from singles play. Here's a concise breakdown of the key rules:

- **Serving Order:** In doubles, each team serves two consecutive points. The service must start from the right half of the table and then alternate between the players. The order of serve (who serves first and second) is determined before the match. This means that your team will have a designated order for serving, which must be maintained throughout the match.

- **Serve and Receive Placement:** The ball must bounce on the right half of the server's side and then cross over the net to the receiver's right half. The diagonal placement ensures fairness and challenges the receiver to cover more distance. Additionally, in doubles, the receiver can return the serve on either side of the table, adding an element of strategy to the game.

- **Let Service:** As in singles, if the ball touches the net during service but still goes over to the other side, it's considered a "let," and the serve is retaken. There is no limit on the number of "lets," but a series of consecutive "lets" can slow down the game's pace.

- **Change of Ends:** Players switch sides when an odd number of games have been played—after the first game and every two games thereafter. This change accounts for any lighting or air circulation variations in different parts of the playing area, ensuring fairness throughout the match.

Team Dynamics: The Heart of Doubles Play

Doubles table tennis is about maintaining synergy with your partner. Team dynamics set it apart from singles, and understanding these dynamics is pivotal to success.

- **Communication:** Effective communication is the cornerstone of successful doubles play. Use verbal and non-verbal cues to coordinate your moves and strategy. Clear communication is vital to keep the game flowing seamlessly, whether a quick shout to signal a switch in positioning or a nod to indicate your readiness to attack. Building a strong rapport with your partner is the key to this aspect. Over time, you'll develop an unspoken understanding of each other's intentions and movements.

- **Covering the Table:** Efficient court coverage is essential. Ensure you and your partner move harmoniously to cover the entire table and avoid open gaps. When one player moves to cover a particular area, the other should adjust their position to account for the vacated space. Effective footwork is crucial, allowing you to transition smoothly between offense and defense and protecting the entire table.

- **Supporting Each Other:** Be a supportive partner. Encourage your teammate, boost morale, and help them regain focus in challenging moments. The mental aspect of doubles play is often underestimated. When one of you faces a rough patch, it's the role of the other to provide support and motivation. Positivity is contagious, and your partner's morale significantly impacts their performance.

- **Predicting Movements:** Understanding your partner's style and anticipating their movements will improve coordination. If your partner favors a backhand stroke, be ready to cover the forehand area. Predicting your partner's next move allows you to make quick positioning and shot selection decisions. This skill becomes increasingly valuable when you both need to switch positions or decide who should take a certain shot.

- **Dividing Roles:** Determine who will play the role of the aggressive attacker and who will focus on consistent blocks and counterattacks. Team roles can change depending on the situation. This aspect is particularly critical when dealing with opponents with distinct playing styles. In some instances, one player may excel at offensive shots like spins and smashes, while the other may have better control and defensive capabilities. Recognizing each other's strengths allows you to adapt your roles to maximize your team's performance.

In doubles play, it's not enough to understand the rules. You must also be in harmony with your partner. Effective communication, court coverage, and role division are the core elements of successful team dynamics.

Thriving in Doubles Play

Now that you have a grasp of the rules and the dynamics of playing in a team take a look at some strategies and techniques to make your partnership a formidable force in the world of doubles table tennis.

Effective Service and Receive Strategies

Serving and receiving effectively sets the tone of a doubles match. Here are strategies to consider:

- **Serve Variety:** Experiment with different types of serves. Vary spin, speed, and placement to keep your opponents guessing. A common tactic in doubles is to use a serve that sets up your partner for an aggressive follow-up shot. For example, a short backspin serve can entice the receiver to push the ball back, setting up an opportunity for your partner to attack. Conversely, a deep and fast serve may force the receiver into a defensive return, allowing you to take control of the rally.

- **Serve and Attack:** Coordinate with your partner to execute serves that set up your team for aggressive follow-up shots. This means understanding each other's strengths and preferences. If your partner excels at aggressive forehand shots, you may want to serve in a way that encourages a return that sets up a forehand opportunity. Effective communication is crucial here, as your partner needs to be ready to capitalize on the setup created by your serve.

- **Receiving Strategy:** Develop a clear plan for receiving services. Depending on their strengths, communicate with your partner about who should return the service. The receiver's role in doubles is to receive the serve effectively and create an advantageous situation for their partner. This could involve a short return to set up your partner's attack, a deep push to force a high return, or a flick to catch the opponents off guard.

Understanding Opponent Strategies

In doubles, it's not just about your partner but also about understanding your opponents. Here's how you can adapt:

- **Recognize Opponent Weaknesses:** Identify the weaker player on the opposing team and exploit their shortcomings. To do this effectively, pay attention to the opponents' playing styles and adapt your strategies accordingly. If one of your opponents struggles with receiving serves with heavy spin, consider targeting them with spin serves. Similarly, if an opponent has a weaker backhand, focus your attacks more on that side.

- **Counteract Strong Shots:** If an opponent has a powerful attack, work with your partner to block and counteract effectively. Facing opponents with strong attacking shots can be challenging, but it's also an opportunity to showcase your blocking and counterattacking skills. By practicing quick and controlled blocks, you can neutralize your opponent's attacks and potentially turn the tables in your favor. Effective communication with your partner is essential in these situations, as you need to coordinate your blocking and counterattacks to maximize their effectiveness.

Team-Based Shot Placement

In doubles, shot placement takes on fresh challenges. Aim for these strategic areas:

- **Wide Angles:** Target wide angles to make it difficult for your opponents to cover the table. Wide-angle shots stretch your opponents' movements and create openings in their defense. If one of your opponents is out of position, a well-placed wide-angle shot can exploit that gap and secure a point for your team.

- **Middle Placement:** Shots placed in the middle of the table can cause confusion between opponents and lead to indecision. When both opponents are uncertain about who should take a shot, it often results in miscommunication or hesitation. This momentary confusion can give your team an advantage. In particular, aim for the crossover point between your opponents. It's the area where the ball is equidistant from both players and, therefore, more challenging to return.

- **Placement Based on Role:** Coordinate with your partner to ensure that your shots complement each other's roles in the team. If your partner is the primary attacker, your role may involve setting them up with strategic placements. For example, you could aim your shots to draw the opponents out of position, creating opportunities for your partner to execute powerful attacks. Conversely, if your partner excels at controlling the rally, you may focus on precise placements that force errors from the opponents. Effective placement requires understanding your partner's role and adapting to the match's ever-changing dynamics.

Quick Switches and Communication

Doubles play is fast-paced, and quick decisions are crucial. Here's how you can master this aspect:

- **Switching Sides:** In response to the ball's trajectory, be ready to switch positions with your partner to maintain optimal positioning. This maneuver often occurs when your team transitions from an offensive phase to a defensive one or vice versa. For example, if you and your partner are both on the offensive and the opponent returns a powerful shot that forces one of you into a defensive position, a quick switch can help maintain the balance. Effective switching minimizes gaps in your court coverage and ensures you're always ready to handle the next shot.

- **Clear Communication:** Use short, clear calls or cues to inform your partner about their role and to avoid collisions. Verbal communication should be concise and specific to the situation. Simple calls like "mine," "yours," or "switch" convey crucial information without confusion. Non-verbal cues, such as hand signals or nods, can also effectively communicate your intentions. The key is to maintain a continuous dialogue with your partner, ensuring you're both on the same page throughout the match.

Reacting to Lobs

Lob shots can disrupt your offensive flow. Develop strategies to handle these situations:

- **Calling for Assistance:** If your partner is better positioned to handle a lob, communicate and allow them to take the shot. Lobs can be tricky, especially if they force you out of your ideal attacking position. In such cases, letting your partner take over is often more effective. A simple call like "yours" or "help" can signal to your partner that you need their assistance handling the lob.

- **Positioning for Lobs:** Work on your positioning to be prepared for lobs and return them effectively. While it's generally the player closest to the net who should handle lobs, there may be situations where the player farther from the net is better positioned to make the return. This decision depends on factors such as your proximity to the ball, your partner's readiness, and your overall court coverage. Practice reading the trajectory of lobs and positioning yourself accordingly to ensure you're always ready to respond.

Thriving in doubles play demands effective service and receive strategies, adaptability to opponent styles, precise shot placement, quick switches, and clear communication. By mastering these techniques, you can make your partnership a formidable force on the doubles table.

Doubles play in table tennis is a unique and thrilling experience where the synergy between you and your partner takes center stage. Understanding the rules, nurturing effective team dynamics, and mastering strategies are the stepping stones to success in this symphony of teamwork. So, embrace the exhilarating journey of doubles play, synchronize your moves with your partner, and let teamwork take your table tennis performance to new heights.

Chapter 7: Scoring and Keeping Tracks

In table tennis, a match is not just a battle of strokes and spins. It's also a cerebral duel where the precise track of the score is essential. In this chapter, you'll unravel the complexities of table tennis scoring, from the rules that govern it to valuable tips on how to keep score accurately. Understanding the scoring system brings harmony to the game and ensures fair play.

Understanding Table Tennis Scoring

Table tennis scoring may appear straightforward at first, but there are nuances and intricacies that you must grasp to appreciate the flow of a match fully.

Scoring System Overview

Table tennis uses a simple and easy-to-understand scoring system. The first player (or team) to reach a predetermined number of points wins a game. Traditionally, the goal is to reach eleven points, and the winning player needs to do so with a 2 point margin. However, in recent years, a new scoring system has been introduced, often called the "11-up" system, where the game is played to 11 points, and a margin of two points is not required for victory.

Serving and Receiving

The server begins each point by serving the ball to the receiver. After every two points, the serve alternates between the players (or teams). In doubles play, each player serves two consecutive points, and then the opponents take their turn to serve. The server must execute a legal serve, ensuring the ball touches the server's right half of the table, then crosses over the net to bounce on the receiver's right half.

Winning a Point

To win a point in table tennis, a player must successfully rally with their opponent and cause the ball to land in the opponent's playing area. The ball must strike the opponent's playing surface, including the table's edges, without touching the net or any part of the surroundings.

Points are scored through a combination of successful serves that lead to winning shots (such as an ace) and rallies where one player fails to return the ball within the rules. Points can be won through various shots, including smashes, loops, and well-placed pushes. Each successful rally results in a point awarded to the player who wins the rally.

Deuce and Advantage

When the score reaches 10-10 (or in the "11-up" system, 10-10 or any tie score), it is referred to as a "deuce." A player must secure a two-point lead to win the game. For example, if the score is 10-10, a player must reach 12 points to win the game as long as the other player does not gain any points. In the "11-up" system, the game can be won by a single point, even at 10-10—a player can win 11-10.

Game and Match Scoring

In a table tennis match, players compete in games, and the first player (or team) to win a specified number of games secures victory. The number of games needed to win a match can vary, but it is typically odd. In many cases, it's the best of 5 or 7 games. A player wins a match by winning the required number of games first. Each game is a separate entity, and winning a game earns you one point towards winning the match.

Score Announcements

The score is typically announced in table tennis, with the server's score mentioned first and the receiver's score second. For example, if the score is 5-3, the server has 5 points, and the receiver has 3 points. This notation is important for players and spectators to keep track of the match's progress.

Understanding table tennis scoring is like learning the notes of a musical score. You must grasp the rules, serving order, and how points are won. This knowledge is foundational to keeping score accurately and enjoying the game.

Tips for Keeping Score Accurately

As vital as understanding the scoring system is, keeping score accurately is equally essential. Precise scorekeeping ensures fair play, minimizes disputes, and allows you to enjoy the game without interruptions. Here are some valuable tips for keeping score with confidence:

15. A scoreboard can help you accurately keep track of the score. Source: Pierre-Yves Beaudouin / Wikimedia Commons: https://commons.wikimedia.org/wiki/File:Mondial_Ping_-_Men%27s_Doubles_-_Semifinals_-_31.jpg

- **Use a Scoreboard:** A scorekeeping tool, such as a scoreboard, is immensely helpful. Traditional scoreboards have sliding markers that indicate the score for both players (or teams). Using a scoreboard eliminates the risk of miscounting or forgetting the score and provides a visual reference for players and spectators.

- **Double-check the Score:** At the end of each point, it's good practice for both the server and the receiver to double-check the score. Verbalizing the score or confirming it with your opponent helps prevent scoring errors. For instance, a quick confirmation can resolve the discrepancy if the server thinks the score is 7-4 while the receiver believes it's 7-3.

- **Focus on the Server's Score:** When announcing the score, it's customary to begin with the server's score. This practice can help minimize confusion and ensure that both players are on the same page regarding the score. For example, saying "7-4" means the server has 7 points, and the receiver has 4.

- **Communicate Clearly:** Effective communication is key to accurate scorekeeping. Use clear and concise language when announcing the score. For example, avoid vague terms like "it's my serve" and instead state the specific score, e.g., "5-3, my serve." Clarity in communication leaves no room for ambiguity.

- **Check after Each Rally:** Make it a habit to confirm the score after each rally, especially when there's a crucial point or doubt. Verifying the score becomes even more critical when the game is close, and a single point can change the outcome. Take a moment to announce the score and ensure you and your opponent agree.

- **Use Gestures and Scorecards:** In addition to verbal communication, you can use hand signals and scorecards to indicate the score. It's advantageous in noisy or crowded environments where verbal communication is challenging. Simple gestures, such as raising the appropriate number of fingers, can convey the score accurately.

- **Maintain Focus:** Maintaining focus is crucial during scorekeeping. Distractions or casual scorekeeping can lead to errors. Treat scorekeeping as seriously as you would your shots. Keep your attention on the game, and don't let your guard down when recording the score.

- **Resolve Discrepancies Amicably:** If a disagreement arises regarding the score, handle it with sportsmanship. Engage in a calm discussion with your opponent, and if necessary, consult with any neutral observers. The goal is to reach a fair resolution and continue the game with clarity and accuracy.

- **Practice Scorekeeping:** The more you practice scorekeeping, the better you become at it. Whether you're playing competitive matches or friendly games, take the opportunity to hone your scorekeeping skills. Practice ensures that you confidently keep score without disruption.

Accurate scorekeeping is the backbone of a fair and enjoyable table tennis match. Implementing these tips, such as using a scoreboard, communicating clearly, and double-checking the score after each point, will enhance your scorekeeping abilities and elevate your table tennis experience.

As you embark on your table tennis journey, armed with the knowledge of scoring and scorekeeping, you're ready to confidently step up to the table. Whether you're playing an intense match or a friendly game, remember that the scoreboard is your guide, your compass through the game. So, keep your wits sharp, your gestures precise, and your focus unwavering.

Chapter 8: Improving Your Game

As you reach the final chapter of this table tennis guide, you're at a pivotal point in your journey. You've learned the basics, understood the rules, and even ventured into doubles and singles play. Now, it's time to explore how to elevate your skills, striving for mastery. In this chapter, you'll discover practical drills and exercises to sharpen your abilities. You'll also explore the value of joining the vibrant table tennis community, a supportive network that can inspire and nurture your passion for the game.

Drills and Exercises for Skill Improvement

16. Drills and exercises can help you improve your skills. Source: https://www.pexels.com/photo/man-playing-table-tennis-14527385/

Table tennis, a sport known for its speed, precision, and finesse, requires continuous practice and skill development to excel. Whether you're a beginner aiming to sharpen your basics or an intermediate player striving for mastery, incorporating targeted drills and exercises into your training routine is essential.

Warm-up Drills

Before diving into the more intricate drills, it's essential to warm up properly. A good warm-up increases blood flow to your muscles, reduces the risk of injuries, and helps you focus. Here are some warm-up exercises:

- **Shadow Play:** Stand by the table and practice your strokes without a ball. This drill helps improve your footwork and shot placement.

- **Footwork Exercises:** Perform ladder drills, side shuffles, and cone drills to enhance your agility and court coverage.

- **Stretching Routine:** Stretch your legs, arms, and core muscles to increase flexibility and reduce the risk of strain.

Fundamental Drills

These drills are suitable for beginners and those looking to reinforce the basics of table tennis.

- **Forehand and Backhand Drives:** Practice these fundamental shots with a partner or against a wall to improve accuracy and consistency. Focus on your stance, grip, and stroke technique.

- **Serve and Receive Drills:** Work on your serving and receiving skills. Vary the placement, spin, and speed of your serves to simulate real-match scenarios. You can also practice reading your opponent's serves.

- **Controlled Placement:** Place a target (like a small box) on the table and aim to consistently hit the ball into that target. This improves your shot accuracy and ball placement.

- **Multi-Ball Drills:** Have a practice partner feed you multiple balls quickly. This will enhance your reflexes, shot selection, and consistency.

Advanced Drills

For intermediate and advanced players, these drills will challenge your skills and push you to the next level.

- **Random Placement:** Have a training partner return your shots randomly to different table areas. This drill improves your adaptability and responsiveness.

- **Counterlooping Drills:** Practice counterlooping against heavy topspin balls. It helps you develop a strong offensive game and neutralize aggressive shots from your opponent.

- **Footwork and Simulated Match Play:** Engage in drills that simulate real match situations. Move around the table to practice shots and scenarios, including forehand and backhand rallies.

Mental Conditioning Exercises

Table tennis is not just a physical game but a mental battle. Strengthen your mental resilience with these exercises:

- **Visualization:** Close your eyes and visualize yourself playing a perfect game. This exercise enhances mental imagery and helps in anticipating your opponent's moves.

- **Meditation:** Meditation improves your focus and concentration. Incorporate mindfulness exercises into your training routine to stay calm under pressure.

- **Match Simulations:** Play practice matches to develop your competitive edge. This will expose you to real match pressure and help you improve your mental composure.

Conditioning and Strength Training

Physical fitness is a crucial aspect of table tennis. These exercises can help you improve your strength, speed, and endurance:

- **Cardio Workouts:** Engage in cardio exercises such as running, swimming, or cycling to enhance your fitness and stamina.

- **Plyometric Exercises:** Incorporate exercises like box jumps and agility ladder drills to improve your explosiveness and agility.

- **Strength Training:** Use weightlifting or bodyweight exercises to strengthen your legs, core, and upper body. A strong core is particularly important for table tennis.

Cool-Down and Recovery

After a rigorous training session, it's essential to cool down and promote recovery:

- **Stretching:** Perform static stretches to relax your muscles and improve flexibility. Focus on areas like the hamstrings, shoulders, and lower back.

- **Hydration:** Rehydrate with water or an electrolyte drink to replenish fluids lost during training.

- **Self-Massage:** Use foam rollers or massage sticks to reduce muscle soreness and improve circulation.

Table tennis is a sport that combines finesse, speed, and strategy. Improving your skills requires a well-rounded approach encompassing technique, mental strength, and physical conditioning. You will become a more formidable table tennis player by incorporating these drills and exercises into your training regimen. Whether you're playing for fun or aiming for competitive success, consistent practice and a commitment to improvement are the keys to your success.

Joining the Table Tennis Community

Table tennis is a vibrant and inclusive community. Being part of this community can enhance your journey as a player, providing you with support, resources, and a shared passion for the game.

Online Video Tutorials:

- **PingSkills:** PingSkills offers a vast collection of free video tutorials on table tennis, from basic techniques to advanced strategies.

- **EmRatThich Table Tennis Coach:** EmRatThich provides detailed video analyses of professional players, breaking down their techniques and tactics.

- **Table Tennis Daily:** This YouTube channel offers match highlights, player interviews, and instructional videos for players of all levels.

Table Tennis Books:

- **"Table Tennis Tactics for Thinkers" by Larry Hodges:** This book delves into the tactical aspects of the game and is highly regarded for its insights into strategy.

- **"Table Tennis: Steps to Success" by Richard McAfee:** This comprehensive guide covers everything from basic techniques to advanced strategies.

Online Forums and Communities:

- **MyTableTennis.NET:** This forum is a hub for table tennis enthusiasts to discuss everything related to the sport. You can find advice, reviews, and answers to your questions here.

- **Table Tennis Daily Forum:** This community forum is another great place to connect with fellow players, ask for advice, and share your experiences.

Mobile Apps:

- **Table Tennis Touch:** This mobile app offers an enjoyable and realistic table tennis experience. It's great for practicing your skills on the go.

- **Ping Pong Masters:** Another fun mobile game that allows you to play table tennis in various settings and improve hand-eye coordination.

Coaching and Training Centers:

- Consider joining a local table tennis club or training center. Professional coaches provide personalized guidance and training.

Table Tennis Organizations:

- Explore websites and resources provided by national and international table tennis organizations. For example, USA Table Tennis (USATT) offers a wealth of information, including coaching resources and event calendars.

Table Tennis Equipment Reviews:

- When you're ready to purchase equipment, consult online reviews and resources like Table Tennis Database (Tabletennisdb.com) to learn about various blades, rubbers, and accessories.

Video Analysis Software:

- To improve your game, consider using video analysis software like "Ping Pong Coach" or "Hudl Technique." These tools allow you to record and analyze your gameplay.

Podcasts:

- Listen to table tennis podcasts, such as "The Expert Table Tennis Podcast" by Ben Larcombe. These podcasts feature interviews with top players and coaches, providing valuable insights into the game.

Professional Matches:

- Watch professional table tennis matches to observe high-level play. Websites like ITTF (International Table Tennis Federation) or YouTube channels dedicated to table tennis matches offer a wide selection.

Remember that improving in table tennis takes practice and dedication. Utilize a combination of these resources to build a strong foundation and refine your skills over time. Whether you're a beginner or an experienced player, the world of table tennis offers a wealth of knowledge and opportunities for growth.

As you conclude this guide, you're not reaching the end but standing at the threshold of an unending journey into table tennis. The path to mastery is an ongoing exploration marked by practice, learning, and camaraderie with fellow players.

By embracing the drills and exercises for skill improvement and joining the table tennis community, you're on the right track to excel in this beautiful sport. Remember that in table tennis, as in life, the journey is as rewarding as the destination. So, let your paddle be your guide, your training your compass, and your fellow players your companions on this exciting adventure.

Conclusion

In your journey from a curious beginner to a confident table tennis player, you've explored the vibrant world of this dynamic sport, learning fundamental techniques, strategies, and even the intricacies of teamwork in doubles play. With each chapter, you've gained essential knowledge and practical skills to play and enjoy table tennis.

Key Takeaways:

1. Getting Started

- Table tennis is an accessible and fun sport for players of all ages and skill levels.
- Understanding the basics, such as the table dimensions and rules, is crucial for a successful start.

2. Essential Equipment

- Your choice of racket, balls, and the playing surface significantly affects your gameplay.
- Selecting equipment that suits your style is key to maximizing your potential.

3. Grips and Strokes

- Mastering different racket grips and basic strokes, like the forehand and backhand, is essential for precise and powerful shots.

- Regular practice and proper form are the foundations of developing your skills.

4. Serving and Receiving

- Serving is your opportunity to set the pace and control the game.

- Effective receiving is about adapting to different serves and positioning yourself for the best returns.

5. Single Play

- Singles matches require not only technical proficiency but also strategic thinking.

- Adapting your game and developing your mental resilience is critical for success.

6. Double Play

- Doubles play introduces a new dimension of teamwork and communication.

- Understanding the rules, team dynamics, and effective strategies will make you a formidable doubles player.

7. Scoring and Keeping Tracks

- Scoring in table tennis is straightforward, but paying attention to the serving order and rules is crucial.

- Keeping track of your progress and analyzing your performance will aid in improvement.

8. Improving Your Game

- Regular practice, using the right drills and exercises, is the path to skill enhancement.

- Physical and mental conditioning, proper warm-up, and recovery routines play significant roles in your development.

This guide has introduced you to the wonderful world of table tennis and equipped you with the knowledge and skills to pursue your passion with confidence and enjoyment. Whether challenging yourself to fierce singles battles or reveling in the art of doubles harmony, the journey of improvement in table tennis is endlessly rewarding.

Have you found this guide helpful in becoming a table tennis enthusiast? Please consider leaving a review and sharing your experience with fellow readers. Good luck on your journey to mastering the art of table tennis. May your rallies be swift and your serves ace-worthy.

References

(N.d.-a). Pingsunday.com. https://pingsunday.com/table-tennis-tricks-for-beginners/

(N.d.-b). Tabletennisarena.com. https://tabletennisarena.com/how-to-play-table-tennis/

10 key tips to advance your table tennis game. (n.d.). Newgy. https://www.newgy.com/pages/10-tips-to-advance-your-table-tennis-game

Bruce, D. (2022, April 13). The ultimate beginners guide to table tennis. Racket Insight. https://racketinsight.com/table-tennis/beginners-guide/

How to play ping pong (table tennis). (2006, September 12). WikiHow. https://www.wikihow.com/Play-Ping-Pong-(Table-Tennis)

How to play table tennis (in 12 simple steps). (2013, March 15). Expert Table Tennis. https://www.experttabletennis.com/how-to-play-table-tennis/

Jamwal, S. (2023, April 17). Table tennis rackets for beginners: Affordable picks for you - Times of India (October, 2023). The Times of India; Times Of India. https://m.timesofindia.com/most-searched-products/sports-equipment/table-tennis-rackets-for-beginners-affordable-picks-for-you/articleshow/99562127.cms

Ramachandran, K. (2023, April 9). Master table tennis: A comprehensive guide for beginners. Tennisgyan.com. https://tennisgyan.com/table-tennis-beginners-guide/

Rees, D. (2021, April 16). 10 Table Tennis Tips for Beginners. Kettler Official Site. https://www.kettler.co.uk/blog/10-table-tennis-tips-for-beginners

Sandoval, E. (2019, June 10). 15 table tennis tips for beginners. Ping Pong Ruler. https://pingpongruler.com/table-tennis-tips/

Ttdementor, W. by. (2017, August 12). Table Tennis — Going from beginner to intermediate level. Medium. https://medium.com/@ttdementor/table-tennis-going-from-beginner-to-intermediate-level-20a059b0806a